LATIMER STUDIES 64

A Step Too Far:

An Evangelical Critique of Christian Mysticism

by Marian Raikes

The Latimer Trust

© Marian Raikes 2006

ISBN 0-946307-58-X

EAN 9780946307586

Published by the Latimer Trust

PO Box 26685

London N14 4XQ

www.latimertrust.org

Contents

Frontispiece: St John Climacus, *The Ladder of Divine Ascent*.
St. Catherine's Monastery, Sinai.

Introduction

Mysticism: the very word provokes a reaction. For conservative (or 'classic') evangelicals, the reaction is usually negative. Suspicion that any reality behind the word will be vague and nebulous, with experience taking priority over belief, and little solid grounding in the Word of God. Suspicion of its Roman Catholic ancestry and its many pre- or counter-Reformation practitioners.

But for most beyond conservative evangelicalism, and for many ordinary folk in conservative churches, precisely the opposite is the case. 'Mysticism' to them is immensely attractive, especially when included in the broader concept of 'spirituality'. It speaks of freedom and adventure, exploration into the spiritual unknown – the 'mysterious', and thereby the possibility of a personal fulfilment not yet found with a 'safer', more conventional evangelical spirituality.

For some, opportunities arise to turn the attraction into action. From friends in another church perhaps, or from a book on their church bookstall[1], they hear about people, whether contemporary or of bygone ages, who appear to have known precisely that greater, more exciting, more joyful intimacy with the Lord which they so desire. They discover the mystics.

Mysticism offers every individual a 'real' encounter with God (or 'Ultimate Reality'), leading to a profound relationship with God accompanied by ecstatic joy. What's

---

[1] See chapter 1 for a survey of 'mystical' literature currently influencing evangelicals.

more, each individual's experience has its own built-in validity. Read the following brief extracts, and consider the undoubted attractiveness to spiritual 'searchers' of what is on offer:

From the English mystic Richard Rolle:

> 'I can declare that contemplation is a wonderful enjoying of the love of God, and this joy is a worship of God which cannot be described. And that amazing worship happens within the soul, and because of the overflowing joy and sweetness, it rises up to the mouth, so that the heart and voice combine in unison, and the body and soul rejoice in the living God.'[2]

Or from a 21st century form of Ignatius' *Spiritual Exercises*:

> 'Through the steps below you can experience this 'method' of growing in a sense of self and the source of self. You can grow more sensitive to your own spirit – its longings, its powers, its Source; and you will develop an openness to receive the support God offers.'[3]

Mysticism is attractive to some because it doesn't demand any great intellectual ability or understanding. It invites us to go 'beyond' the verbal and cerebral pursuits which characterise classic evangelical spirituality (Bible studies, prayer meetings, expository sermons, 'Quiet Times' etc.). Similarly, for those of a more introverted disposition, the emphasis on solitude and silence may be a welcome respite from the (to them) noisy, stressful 'activism' of much evangelical life. Others are impressed by the fierce passion of so many of the mystics. The ever-popular Julian of Norwich,

---

[2] R. Rolle, *A Form of Living*, in *The English Writings* [ed. Allen], Classics of Western Spirituality, London: SPCK, 1989, ch.12
[3] www.jesuits.ca/spirituality/examen.htm

for example:

> 'Until I am fully one with him, I can never have full rest
> nor true bliss; that is to say, until I am so at one with him
> that no thing created comes between us, my God and me.'[4]

Yet others are drawn by the focus on God's love, or by the promise of a richer and more 'satisfying' prayer life, or by some particular teaching, for example Julian's insistence on the all-accepting nature of God's love which never condemns anyone. For these and many other reasons, a significant number of people who regularly worship in evangelical churches are turning to the mystics to 'supplement' their spirituality.

For their benefit, and for the benefit of their pastors, this little booklet will aim to assess so-called 'Christian' mysticism[5] from a conservative viewpoint, and at the same time to offer some indications of a more biblical alternative. For this writer firmly believes that, objectively speaking, there is never any need to look beyond a truly biblical, evangelical spirituality. Scripture *is* fully sufficient.

I.   A survey of the literature

Too many evangelicals are largely ignorant of who the mystics were or what they wrote and believed about spiritual

---

[4] Julian of Norwich, *Revelations of Divine Love*, [ed. Wolters], London: Penguin, 1966, p.5
[5] I intend to restrict myself largely to Western mysticism, partly for reasons of space and partly because the Eastern mystics do not yet seem to be directly influencing evangelicals to the same extent as, for example, Julian of Norwich, John of the Cross or Ignatius of Loyola.

growth. If that is not true of you, do feel free to skip this section. For those who are still with me, first let me explain that I'm not even going to attempt a complete survey of 'mystical' literature. Instead I will focus on those works which, to a greater or lesser extent, are currently influencing British evangelicals. Therefore, apart from mentioning that there is some 'mystical' content in Augustine's *Confessions*[6], we will bypass the first twelve hundred years of Christian history. Most of the currently popular classic works come from the later medieval period of Western mysticism, and divide broadly into two groups: the English mystics and the Spanish mystics.

The English Mystics are:

(i) the colourful and enthusiastic (some say eccentric) visionary hermit Richard Rolle (c.1290-1349) who wrote *The Fire of Love* and *A Form of Living*.[7]

(ii) Walter [of] Hilton (d. 1396), an academic who wrote *The Scale of Perfection*[8] and *The Mixed Life*.[9] *The Scale of Perfection* describes the reform of the soul in four stages, based on Hilton's interpretation of Romans 8:30.

(iii) Julian of Norwich (c. 1342-1413), a solitary 'anchoress' who lived in a cell attached to St. Julian's church in

---

[6] There are many editions, e.g. *The Confessions of St. Augustine* [trans. E.M. Blaicklock] Hodder & Stoughton, 1983
[7] Richard Rolle, *The Fire of Love* [ed. C. Wolters], London: Penguin Classics, 1972; *A Form of Living* may be found in *The English Writings* [ed. Allen], Classics of Western Spirituality, London: SPCK, 1989
[8] Walter [of] Hilton, *The Scale of Perfection* [ed. Clark & Dorwood], Classics of Western Spirituality, New York: Paulist Press, 1991
[9] *The Mixed Life* may be found in *The Minor Works of Walter Hilton* [ed. Jones], London: Burns & Oates & Washbourne, 1929

Norwich. In 1373, while seriously ill, she experienced a series of sixteen personal 'revelations'. Thereafter she wrote (or perhaps dictated) *Revelations of Divine Love*[10] in both an early, shorter, form and a later, longer, form. The latter incorporates her own reflections upon her experiences and her interpretation of them.

(iv) Margery Kempe (c. 1373-1436), an illiterate and highly emotional housewife from King's Lynn, who dictated the autobiographical *Book of Margery Kempe*.[11]

(v) the anonymous, scholarly, author of *The Cloud of Unknowing*.[12] He was probably a Carthusian monk, and possibly also the author of *The Epistle of Privy Counsel* and *The Epistle on Prayer*. *The Cloud* is highly critical of visionary experiences like those of Julian of Norwich or Richard Rolle.

Of all these, *The Cloud of Unknowing* and Julian's *Revelations of Divine Love* are by far the best known and most widely read. Indeed, the former has been reprinted almost annually since the 1960s.

While the English mystics are all pre-Reformation Catholic writers, the Spanish mystics are all post-Reformation Catholics, offering an alternative spirituality to the Protestantism of Luther and company. The two groups are therefore quite distinct, not only culturally and linguistically, but also historically and theologically.

---

[10] Julian of Norwich, *Revelations of Divine Love*, op. cit.
[11] Margery Kempe, *The Book of Margery Kempe* [ed. Windeatt], London: Penguin Classics, 1985
[12] Anon, *The Cloud of Unknowing* [ed. Walsh], Classics of Western Spirituality, New York: Paulist Press, 1981

The Spanish mystics are:

(i)   Teresa of Avila (1515-1582), a Carmelite nun who often enjoyed mystical visions and 'ecstasies'. Among other works, she wrote *The Interior Castle*[13], the castle being a metaphor for the human soul. The castle has seven 'dwelling places', each with many rooms or gardens, all of which must be travelled through in order to reach union with God at the centre.

(ii)   John of the Cross (1542-1591), another Carmelite (and Teresa's 'Confessor'), who has been called 'Spain's greatest poet.' In addition to the poetry, he wrote four prose works, all commentaries on his poetry. *The Dark Night of the Soul* and *The Ascent of Mount Carmel* comment on a poem called *The Dark Night of the Soul*. *The Living Flame of Love* and *The Spiritual Canticle* comment on poems of the same names.[14]

Not always included in surveys of the Spanish mystics, but certainly a Spaniard who was also a mystic is:

(iii) Ignatius of Loyola (1491-1556) author of *The Spiritual Exercises*.[15] Ignatius was a nobleman and soldier who made a radical commitment to Jesus while convalescing from a leg wound received in battle. After a period of doubt and depression, he received five 'illuminations' and began to write down his

---

[13] Teresa of Avila, *The Interior Castle*, Classics of Western Spirituality, London: SPCK, 1979

[14] E. Allison Peers [trans / ed.] *The Complete Works of St. John of the Cross*, London: Burns, Oates & Washbourne, 1947

[15] There are many editions of the *Exercises*, eg. G.E.Ganss et al [ed.] *Ignatius of Loyola: the Spiritual Exercises and selected works*, New York: Paulist Press, 1991

experiences and reflections. These notes eventually developed into the *Exercises* and became the training manual for his newly founded Order of the Society of Jesus (Jesuits). They detail a four 'week' programme of exercises such as meditations, self-examinations and penances.

Other popular classic writers whose works either contain elements of mysticism or are claimed as 'mystical' by the mystics include:

(iv)   Brother Lawrence (1611-1691), a French Carmelite monk and author of *The Practice of the Presence of God*.[16] His spirituality is particularly attractive to some because it appears to minimise formal worship and church involvement. ('We make a chapel of our hearts.'[17])

(v)   Jonathan Edwards (1703-1758), especially because he describes the results of revival in language very familiar to mystics: 'the soul ... has been ... perfectly overwhelmed, and swallowed up with light and love and a sweet solace, rest and joy of soul that was altogether unspeakable ... the soul remained in a kind of heavenly elysium, and did as it were swim in the rays of Christ's love ...'[18] His theology, however, is of course more Reformed than Roman Catholic, and nowhere does he espouse the threefold 'mystical way' which underlies most 'Christian' mysticism.

---

[16] Brother Lawrence [trans Attwater] *The Practice of the Presence of God*, Springfield: Templegate, 1974
[17] ibid., in the 7th letter.
[18] Jonathan Edwards, *Some Thoughts concerning the Revival*, in *The Works of Jonathan Edwards* [ed. Goen], vol4, New Haven and London, 1972, pp.331-332

Of the modern mystics the most influential must be:

(vi) Evelyn Underhill (1875-1941), who may not be so widely read among evangelicals (perhaps because she rarely mentions God, let alone Jesus), but certainly remains very influential in the wider church. She wrote *Mystics of the Church, Practical Mysticism: a Little Book for Normal People*[19] and other works.

(vii) Thomas Merton (1915-1969), author of *Seeds of Contemplation, Seven Storey Mountain, Contemplative Prayer* and other works. In *Seven Storey Mountain*, he recounts his own spiritual 'journey' from atheism and immorality to the severe life of a Trappist monk.[20]

In addition to all these, there are the many advocates of mysticism, who may or may not be mystics themselves. The 'mystical' archbishops are well known – Michael Ramsay and Rowan Williams. But there are also a significant number of people who recommend mysticism as both credible and helpful specifically to evangelicals. In America, Winfried Corduan has written *Mysticism: an Evangelical Option?*, a question which expects the qualified answer 'yes'.[21] While rightly rejecting the idea that any new truth may be learned through mystical experience, he nonetheless concludes that mysticism is an important aspect of 'uncompromised biblical

---

[19] E. Underhill, *Mystics of the Church*, Cambridge: Clarke, 1925 and *Practical Mysticism: A Little Book for Normal People*, London: Dent, 1919
[20] Thomas Merton, *The Seven Storey Mountain*, San Francisco: Harper & Row, 1984
[21] Winfried Corduan, *Mysticism: An Evangelical Option?* Grand Rapids: Zondervan, 1991; James Houston has also defended mysticism in the not-so-easily accessible *Gott Lieben und seine Gebote halten,* Basle: Brunner Verlag, 1991, pp.163-181

Christianity.'[22]   Bruce Demarest, too, has testified to the 'benefits of discovering mysticism' in *Satisfy your Soul*.[23] In Britain, Alison Fry produced the Grove booklet *Learning from the English Mystics*,[24] and Richard Foster's *Celebration of Discipline* is on many evangelical bookstalls and bookshelves. He advises,

> 'In addition to studying the Bible, do not neglect the study of some of the experiential classics in Christian literature. Begin with *The Confessions* of St Augustine. Next turn to *The Imitation of Christ* by Thomas à Kempis.   Don't neglect *The Practice of the Presence of God* by Brother Lawrence. For an added pleasure read *The Little Flowers of St. Francis* by Brother Ugolino ... Enjoy the *Table Talks* of Martin Luther before you wade into Calvin's *Institutes of the Christian Religion* ... From the twentieth century read *A Testament of Devotion* by Thomas Kelly ...'[25]

Foster himself is a Quaker (as is Thomas Kelly), but there are mystics and advocates of mysticism from all denominations. Indeed, one of the attractions of mysticism is its 'unifying' approach to Christianity, because what unites mystics in terms of experience is seen to be far more important than what may divide in terms of theology. For Christians who have little awareness of theological niceties, and many friends and relations in other denominations, this seems admirable.

---

[22] ibid., p.138
[23] Bruce Demarest, *Satisfy your Soul: Restoring the Heart of Christian Spirituality*, Colorado Springs: NavPress, 1999. Demarest's experience is helpfully quoted in Mike Raiter's *Stirrings of the Soul,* London: Good Book Co, 2003, p.81f
[24] Alison Fry, *Learning from the English Mystics*, Cambridge: Grove Spirituality Series no.68, 1999
[25] R. Foster, *Celebration of Discipline: The Path to Spiritual Growth*, revised edition; San Francisco: Harper & Row, 1988, p.89

Inevitably, the advocates of mysticism highlight all its positive features. The benefits of meditating upon scripture as well as studying it, for example. Although evangelicals do have their own goodly heritage of meditation (in the Puritans), they have largely lost sight of it; few evangelical pastors seem to be either teaching or modelling meditative skills. The mystics' techniques of meditation may not always be acceptable, but the principle of spending time 'mulling over' familiar scripture passages is a good one. Sometimes evangelicals can be too frenetically active. The basic understanding that Christians are meant to grow spiritually, and to take responsibility for their own spiritual growth, is thoroughly biblical, even if the mystical model of spiritual growth is not. Sometimes we can be too complacent, too stagnant. The complete absence of fear with regard to the world of sense, experience and emotion is worth consideration too. The mystics may overemphasise it, but that should not be allowed to provoke evangelicals into altogether devaluing it. Though rightly cautious, sometimes we can be too exclusively cerebral.

There are also some 'positives' specific to particular mystics: Brother Lawrence's emphasis on being able to pray anywhere and in one's own words, for example. Richard Rolle's undeniably passionate love for Jesus. Julian of Norwich's longing to share Christ's suffering. Walter Hilton's insistence that intimacy with God is for every Christian, not just the 'gifted' few. Thomas Merton's understanding that the root of prayer is perpetual surrender to God. From an evangelical point of view, perhaps the most 'positives' are found with Ignatius: his encouragement to open up the scriptures, and read them for oneself; his advice to keep one's meditations Christ-centred; his appreciation of the seriousness of sin; his belief in the benefits of one-to-one spiritual conversation.

These are features of mysticism we can applaud, and from which we can learn, although it has to be said that they were all there in scripture first! But, however much we may desire to learn positively, we must recognise that there are also grave problems and dangers inherent in the very foundations of mysticism. The first are ...

2.   The problems of definition and subjectivity

There is no universal, commonly agreed, definition of mysticism. A wide variety of definitions have been offered: 'an unmediated link to an absolute',[26] 'the art of union with Reality',[27] 'an attitude of mind which seeks to transcend reason and attain a direct experience of God',[28] 'communication with God',[29] 'the quest to attain union with God', and so on. One thing all definitions agree on is that mysticism is concerned with experience rather than belief. In its broadest definition, the word describes any professed experience of God or 'Ultimate Reality', not necessarily Christian.

However, a much more precise definition is that first adopted by William James in 1922. James famously suggested four marks by which to identify a 'mystical' experience.[30] The two most important, and normative, are

---

[26] W. Corduan, *Mysticism: An Evangelical Option?* Grand Rapids: Zondervan, 1991, p.122
[27] E. Underhill, *Practical Mysticism: A Little Book for Normal People*, p.2
[28] M. Smith, *An Introduction to Mysticism*, London: Sheldon, 1977, p.3
[29] M. Cox, *A Handbook of Christian Mysticism* Part 1, Crucible, 1986, p.21, quoting Inge.
[30] W. James, *The Varieties of Religious Experience*, Longmans, 1922

ineffability and noetic quality. Ineffability means that no adequate account of the experience can be given in words; it is ultimately indescribable, too great for words to express. And 'noetic' means the experience conveys some insight into supra-rational truth. James writes:

> 'Mystical states seem to those who experience them to be also states of knowledge ... They are illuminations, revelations, full of significance and importance, all inarticulate though they remain; and as a rule, they carry with them a curious sense of authority for after-time.'[31]

Evelyn Underhill says something similar:

> 'Mysticism, like revelation, is final and personal ... experience in its most intense form ... the soul's solitary adventure ...'[32]

Hence, of the two classic normative features considered necessary to define an experience as mystical, the first is entirely negative, and the second entirely subjective. Yet mystical experiences claim 'a curious sense of authority'. Such statements rightly give evangelicals cause for concern.

If spirituality is to be truly Christian, it must be soundly based on Christian doctrine; it must have a rational content. It is highly dangerous to separate 'mystical' (or 'spiritual') and doctrinal theology. Yet many of the mystics discourage rational thought (in favour of love). Teresa of Avila, for example: 'In order to ... ascend to the dwelling places we desire, the important thing is not to think much but to love much.'[33] Furthermore, many regard creeds as almost irrelevant to the 'reality' of their spiritual encounter

---

[31] ibid., p.380
[32] E. Underhill, *Mysticism*, London: Methuen, 1967, p.82f
[33] Teresa of Avila, *The Interior Castle*, p.70

with God.[34]   Evelyn Underhill's work is a particularly clear example. As Mike Raiter rightly remarks,

> 'For mystics, spirituality is fundamentally about a subjective sense of union with God, not cognitive adherence to objective truths.'[35]

Of course we must beware of limiting Almighty God to the bounds of human rationality.   But scripture is *his* self-revelatory Word, and it is not all vague mystery; its meaning is plain and clear (perspicuous), and it is our sole authority. To have any validity, therefore, a professed 'encounter with God' or an experience based 'revelation' must be submissible to checking by scripture. Too many modern 'mystics' are unwilling to do this, apparently regarding their 'mystical experience' as self-authenticating.[36]

Two further, 'less sharply marked' qualities of a 'mystical' experience are transiency and passivity. These are, according to James, usual characteristics, but not necessarily normative ones. Transiency indicates that the mystical state cannot be sustained beyond (at most) an hour or two. This is reflected in the classic accounts. Passivity refers to the fact that, during a mystical experience, the mystic commonly 'feels as if his own will were in abeyance.' Although certain techniques may be recommended to facilitate an experience, the experience itself happens *to* the mystic; it is not something which he or she can initiate. 'The mystics could teach contemplation, but only God could give the 'mystical'

---

[34] An understandable reaction to the prevailing dry scholasticism of their time; nevertheless, their anti-intellectualism is not helpful to readers today.

[35] M. Raiter, *Stirrings of the Soul*, London: Good Book Co, 2003, p.167

[36] For example, Anthony Duncan, cited in M. Cox, *A Handbook of Christian Mysticism*, p.250ff

experience of union with himself.'[37]

James' four characteristics form by far the most common definition of mysticism currently in use. However, back in the Middle Ages, Christian 'mysticism' simply meant 'direct personal experience of God'. Hence every true Christian was a mystic. Jesus himself was a 'mystic', and has often been so-called. Mysticism was not primarily about techniques but about being preoccupied with God, especially the love of God. The aim was laudable, and, in the context of scholastic Catholicism, very understandable: to know God experientially, not just intellectually. Some still use the term in this way today, including most of those who wish to commend mysticism to evangelicals. Hence the 'mystic' literature is scattered with quotes such as:

> 'To be a mystic is simply to participate here and now in real and eternal life.'[38]

> 'Every real Christian is a mystic in the Pauline sense.'[39]

> 'A mystic ... is a lover of God who pursues the beloved actively and deeply.'[40]

> 'Christians believe that God wishes to dwell in the hearts of all men and women, and Christian mysticism is a mysterious experience of that presence.'[41]

Used in this way, 'mysticism' sounds harmless enough, doesn't it? No wonder so many find it unproblematic.

Furthermore, its advocates profess to find full support

---

[37] Alison Fry, *Learning from the English Mystics*, p.11f
[38] M. Smith, *An Introduction to Mysticism*, p.11, quoting E. Underhill
[39] W. Corduan, *Mysticism: An Evangelical Option?* p.128f, citing Stewart
[40] B. Robertson, *What is a Christian mystic?* On the website www.christianmystics.com
[41] On the website www.pastornet.net.au/jmm/spir

for mysticism in the pages of scripture. Specific 'mystical' experiences are usually traced back to Moses' encounter with the Lord on Mount Sinai (Exodus 19), and may include Elijah's hearing the 'still small voice' (1 Kings 19:13ff), Ezekiel's vision (Ezekiel 1), the experience of Christ's transfiguration (Luke 9:28-36), Paul's encounter with Christ on the Damascus Road (Acts 9:3-9), his being 'caught up to the third heaven' (2 Corinthians 12:1-4) and John's vision of the risen Christ on Patmos (Revelation 1:9-20). Such 'experiences of God' are then taken to be normative and paradigmatic for Christians today. Indeed, Paul in particular is commonly regarded as *the* great biblical exemplar of mysticism.

But this argument merely demonstrates the definition problem, because already 'mystical' experience has been narrowed down from that permanent friendship with God in Christ, which all true Christians experience throughout their lives, to the select, specific, temporary, 'high' experiences of certain key individuals in the Bible. What's more, these individuals are all either prophets, apostles, or even the Son of God himself. That is: they are unique individuals whose unique experiences cannot be taken as paradigmatic for all Christians. A proper study of the passages cited above leads precisely to the opposite conclusion: such experiences are *not* normative for every ordinary believer today.

Of course, we do need to be careful not to throw the baby out with the bathwater. The Bible does not belittle experience; rather it encourages us to *expect* to experience our Lord. Our knowledge of God in Christ is never mere head knowledge; if it is true knowledge at all, then it is experiential knowledge. The same *kind* of knowledge as that between the three persons of the Trinity: loving, intimate, relational knowledge.[42] It is precisely this truth that many of the medieval mystics rightly wish to emphasise. However, though our knowledge of God is relational, it is not, in contrast to classic mystical spirituality, primarily subjective. There *is* a subjective side to our knowing God in Christ; we do experience his steadfast sacrificial love for us, and our emotions are involved in and affected by the relationship with him. Nonetheless, our relational knowledge of God is primarily objective, firmly founded on objective truths concerning Christ's incarnation, life, death, resurrection and ascension.

What's more, for genuine Christians, this experience of God found 'in Christ' can never be transient; it is either for all eternity, or it is not genuine at all. Subjective human emotions are of course transient and changeable, but the objective experience is not. This is why evangelicals are right to be cautious; emotions are not a trustworthy guide to objective reality; indeed, they are too easily manipulated for that. 'High' emotions (joy, exhilaration etc) may not be indications of a 'higher' spiritual state. A charismatic speaker, an intense atmosphere, physical illness (Julian?), fasting, flagellation (Ignatius?) and drugs are just a few of many causes that may produce heightened emotions. Such 'highs' should not be feared, but neither, as many of the mystics themselves warn, should they be over-valued or sought out. Our goal as Christians is the sacrificial obedience of Christlikeness,[43] and that objective will always be more

---

[42] See, for example, John 10:14f; this line of thought is more fully developed in my own *Presenting Everyone Mature*, [Orthos 21], Blackpool: Fellowship of Word and Spirit, 2004

[43] See, for example, Romans 8:29; Ephesians 4:13; Colossians 3:1-10

important than any subjective experience.

In spite of the variety of characters, beliefs, emphases and practices involved, there are certain common themes running through the 'mystical' literature. Perhaps the most significant of these is the underlying model of spiritual growth, known as the 'mystical way'. Sometimes it is explicit, sometimes simply assumed.

3. The problem of ascent

Mysticism typically sees spirituality as a series of ascending stages. The imagery normally used is that of climbing a ladder or journeying up a mountain. Thus, Walter [of] Hilton called his major work the *Scala Perfectionis* (Ladder of Perfection), and John of the Cross wrote *The Ascent of Mount Carmel*.

Ladder imagery is taken from Jacob's dream of 'a ladder set up on the earth, the top of it reaching to heaven; and the angels of God were ascending and descending on it.'[44] Mountain imagery usually purports to originate with Exodus 19-24 and Moses ascending Mount Sinai to meet with God. Many also refer to the Israelites ascending Mount Zion to worship the Lord, looking especially to Psalms 120-134. In addition, it's regarded as highly significant that Jesus delivered his most famous sermon on a mountain (Matthew 5-7) and revealed his glory on a mountain at the transfiguration (Matthew 17:1-8). McGrath typically comments, 'In each case, the idea of ascent is linked with that

---

[44] Genesis 28:12; In John 1:51, Jesus applies this verse to himself.

of drawing closer to God.'[45]

The mystics are right insofar as the Bible does picture heaven as 'above', and those who move between heaven and earth as ascending or descending.[46] Nonetheless, to use Genesis 28:12 as they do is to misapply it. For a start, it is not humans but angels who ascend and descend Jacob's ladder. And, as to the meaning of the dream, Wenham comments, 'this vision of the angels is an assurance of God's protection of Jacob'.[47] The ladder is not meant to be understood as an image of progressive spiritual growth, or as a guide to mystical union with God. Similarly with the mountain imagery: Moses was the exception to the rule that 'the people are not permitted to come up to Mount Sinai' (Exodus 19:23), and when he did ascend the mountain, it was not for reasons of personal spiritual growth but in order to receive normative revelation for the whole people of God. His unique encounter with God on Sinai cannot simply be equated with our own spiritual experience.

It's hardly surprising, then, that such ascent imagery has been heavily criticised by evangelicals. The mystics had taken a biblical image and used it as a framework for their own ideas; they should have allowed the Bible to define how its own imagery should be interpreted. If they had done so, they would have discovered that scripture uses ascent language to emphasise the holy, almighty nature of the Lord our God. A right response therefore should be the same as

---

[45] Alister McGrath, *Christian Spirituality*, Oxford: Blackwell, p.103
[46] For example, angels in Judges 13:20, Elijah in 2 Kings 2:11, Jesus in Luke 24:51 and Acts 1:9-11. See also Deuteronomy 30:12, Isaiah 14:13, Romans 10:6, Ephesians 4:8-10.
[47] G.J. Wenham, *Word Biblical Commentary* on Genesis 16-50, Dallas: Word, 1994, p.222

that of Jacob and Moses, namely worship.[48]

Inevitably, such 'ascent' language has typically been associated with 'journey' and 'pilgrimage' language in the mystical literature.   In recent years the 'journey' has increasingly tended to be inward as well as upward.[49] Richard Foster, for example, emphasises the importance of the spiritual journey inwards: 'we must be willing to go down into the recreating silences, into the inner world of contemplation.'[50]   There is not the space to engage in a thorough critique of 'journey' language here. Suffice it to say that, when scripture calls believers to be 'pilgrims' or 'sojourners', the emphasis is on the call to live holy lives as aliens and exiles in this world to which we no longer belong. It is not calling us to travel *from* this world *towards* heaven in order to be closer to God. Rather, any true believer is already a citizen of heaven, and we cannot get any closer to God than we already are in Christ.

It is also sometimes claimed that passages such as Ephesians 4:7-16 and Hebrews 5:11-14 support the mystical use of 'ascent' and 'journey' language, indicating the progressive nature of spiritual growth. But these verses support no more than the general concept of spiritual growth; they contain no suggestion of people 'climbing closer' to God, nor of any normative, identifiable 'stages on the way'. Rather, they simply teach that we grow as Christians in the same way as we began – by grace, through faith; by the Word and the

---

[48] See Genesis 28:16-22; Exodus 24ff
[49] Following Plotinus (see p.34ff), who turned Plato's ascent in a more inward direction.
[50] R. Foster, *Celebration of Discipline: The Path to Spiritual Growth*, p.19

Spirit working together to conform us to Christ.[51]

4. The 'Threefold Path'

The number of rungs on the mystical ladder or stages on the spiritual journey varies. The 6th century *Rule of Benedict* described 12 degrees of humility, called 'a ladder of our ascending actions'.[52] At about the same time, John Climacus (579-649) wrote *The Ladder of Divine Ascent*, in 30 chapters corresponding to the 30 rungs on his ladder, one for each year of Christ's life before his baptism. 'Baptised in the 30th year of his earthly age, Christ attained the 30th step on the spiritual ladder'.[53] In spite of the alarming implications of such an assertion, the book has had a massive influence on Eastern orthodoxy. The ladder concept was further developed by the 12th century Carthusian monk Guigo II (1140-1193) in *The Ladder of Monks*. He regarded his four stages of 'spiritual reading' (*'lectio divina'*) as 'a means, like steps on a ladder, by which their user may ascend to higher levels of spiritual awareness'.[54] However the majority of mystics agree on three key stages. The 'mystical way' is therefore also commonly known as 'the threefold path' or 'the triple way'.

It was first formulated, as far as we can tell, by Clement of Alexandria (c.150-214) in *Stromateis 5* and by Origen (c.185-254) in his *Commentary on the Song of Songs*,

---

[51] See also Galatians 3:1-5; Colossians 2:6f
[52] *The Rule of Benedict*, [trans J. McCann] London: Sheed & Ward, 1976, ch.7
[53] John Climacus, *The Ladder of Divine Ascent, Classics of Western Spirituality*, London: SPCK, 1982, p.291
[54] Guigo II, *The Ladder of Monks II*; available at www.ldysinger.com

from a mixture of scriptural texts[55] and neoplatonic ideas. The basic idea was that the soul must embark on an upward journey toward recovering the likeness of God. First, it must be purified through the practice of moral virtues, then it must learn to contemplate God's created world (especially light), and finally it would arrive at the vision of God and union with Him.[56] Origen associated these three stages with beginners (*praxis*), proficients (*theoria*) and the perfect (*theologia*). Many other major themes of later Christian mysticism are also found in his writings.[57]

In the East, Gregory of Nyssa's (c.335-395) *Life of Moses* described the ascent by stages to encounter with God in terms of the contemplation of darkness rather than light, using Moses' ascent of Mount Sinai as a metaphor. For him, the ascent climaxes in an encounter with darkness, an encounter in which God is experienced, but never truly known because he is finally unknowable. This approach is called an 'apophatic' understanding of mystical contemplation and union, in contrast to Origen's more kataphatic understanding (in which contemplation focuses on the created order, especially light, and final union is more static and perfect). Although kataphatic mysticism is becoming more popular today, it is the apophatic kind which has had the deeper and more lasting effect on mystical theology.

Also in the 4th century, Evagrius of Pontus (344-399)

---

[55] For example, Ephesians 4:11-24, Luke 20:36

[56] The 'threefold path' is summarised by Peter Tyler in *The New SCM Dictionary of Christian Spirituality*, [ed. Sheldrake] London: SCM, 2005, p.626f

[57] For example, the love of God, the knowledge of God, and the relationship between contemplation and action.

was combining Origen's theology of spiritual growth with the ascetic teachings of the Desert Fathers, especially their thinking on purification and spiritual warfare.[58] This combination led him to assume that the mystical life must presuppose the monastic life. Only in such a context of withdrawal from the world could the soul properly engage in spiritual warfare, subduing the passions and overcoming temptations. Thus, from the 4th century onwards, monasticism was the context for most forms of mysticism until the 12th century.

The long association with monasticism resulted in the very unhelpful separation of Christians into 'classes'. Those pursuing the mystic way within the monasteries were regarded as living the ideal Christian life; those ordinary folk outside could only hope to experience, at best, what Raiter calls 'a lower level of intimacy with God.'[59] Some, like Benedict, said quite explicitly that one could be a better Christian in 'the religious life' than one could outside it. This unbiblical tendency to 'classify' Christians was compounded by the division within mysticism into beginners, proficients and perfects, and by the concept of 'the mystical faculty' as a special divine gift. Sadly, the tendency still persists, with many writers apparently viewing mystics as on a higher spiritual plane than 'ordinary' Christians. Evelyn Underhill is probably the most prominent modern example, maintaining that 'the special mystic sense differs from and transcends the emotional, intellectual and volitional life of ordinary men.'[60]

---

[58] See his Treatise on Prayer in J.E. Bamberger *Evagrius Ponticus: Prakticos and Chapters on Prayer*, Cistercian Studies 4, Kalamazoo WI: Cistercian Publications, 1981

[59] M. Raiter, *Stirrings of the Soul*, p.181

[60] E. Underhill *Mysticism*, pp.73-82

Meanwhile, in the west, Augustine (354-430) was writing his *Confessions*, recounting his own 'high' experiences of God, and preaching on the mystical dimensions of the psalms. These works, plus his teaching on the relationship between the Trinity and the soul and his analysis of various kinds of visionary experience, were all formative in shaping many later forms of mysticism. John Cassian (c.360-435) too was influential, doing for the western church what Evagrius did for the eastern. He combined Origenic theology with desert asceticism, writing of purity of heart as the way to true ('fiery and wordless') contemplation.

Then, in the 5th century, an unknown writer known pseudonymously as Dionysius the Areopagite outlined yet another programme of ascent to God based on Moses' ascent of Mount Sinai. It began with the (necessary but insufficient) kataphatic use of words, symbols, liturgies and positive assertions about God, then led into an apophatic mysticism in which only negatives can be used of God and the soul ultimately finds Him in the 'utter darkness' of silence and unknowing. Pseudo-Dionysius' *Mystical Theology* was translated and introduced to the west in the 9th century by the Irish scholar John Scotus Erigena, and it has remained enormously influential ever since. [61] Pseudo-Dionysius also renamed the three stages of the (by now well established) ascent as they would come to be known from then on: first the way of purification or purgation, then the way of illumination and finally the way of union.

The 12th century saw the climax of monasticism and the rise of a new form of mysticism, no longer based on

---

[61] *Pseudo-Dionysius: The Complete Works* [trans Luibheid], Classics of Western Spirituality, New York: Paulist Press, 1987

withdrawal from the world, and open to all Christians, including women and the uneducated classes. Francis of Assisi (1182-1226), with his 'four cornerstones' of humility, simplicity, poverty and prayer, became the image of the ideal mystic. For a while the focus was more on personal accounts of visionary experiences than on systematised programmes for spiritual growth. Bernard of Clairvaux had to warn of the need for such testimonies to be in accord with scripture. The Franciscan Bonaventure (1221-1274) again outlined the 'classic spiritual itinerary', this time detailing the content of the three paths.[62]

The 14th and 15th centuries were characterised by endless debates over true and false mysticism, focusing especially on the relationship between the individual mystic and the church. Then, in the 16th century, John of the Cross produced the most systematic analysis yet of the threefold way. Using the metaphor of climbing Mount Carmel, he viewed the 'ascent' as a journey away from a devotional life based on the senses, through various 'nights' of sensory deprivation, purification and spiritual darkness, to the 'summit' of transforming union with God. It is on John of the Cross's work that the following summary of the threefold path is largely based.

(i)   *The way of purification or purgation, also known as 'the state of beginners',[63] during which the soul aims to be freed from the pull of the senses by means of mortification, self-denial and self-discipline.*

---

[62] See his *Journey of the Mind into God* (*Itinerarium Mentis in Deum*), in *The Works of St. Bonaventure* [ed. P. Boehner & Z. Hayes] vol 2, revd ed., New York: Franciscan Institute Publications, 2002
[63] John of the Cross, *Ascent of Mount Carmel* 2:17

The Cloud of Unknowing explains how to begin upon this way: 'There are certain preparatory exercises which should occupy the attention of the contemplative apprentice: the lesson, the meditation and the petition. They may be called, for better understanding, reading, reflecting and praying.'[64]

The subject matter for reading and meditation would chiefly be the scriptures, but other devotional works, especially the lives of the saints, might also aid mortification and inspire contemplation. Bonaventure encourages meditation on the crucified Christ, in order to nurture and sustain a love for Christ. Walter Hilton wisely emphasises the study of scripture as well as reading and meditation, in order to acquire a true knowledge of God.[65] For him, as for Julian, Ignatius, Teresa and many others, the subject matter must be Christ-centred, focusing on our Lord's life, passion and resurrection. Sadly, however, none of them shows much awareness of the need to abide by principles of interpretation such as the importance of meditating on a text in context, of allowing scripture to interpret scripture, or of exegesis rather than eisegesis. Ignatius' encouragement to use the imagination in meditation, while it has undoubted benefits, renders the *Spiritual Exercises* particularly prone to this last danger. The 'beginner' will also use the scriptures, and, in some cases, icons or religious imagery, to assist a right focus in 'discursive prayer', that is the conscious 'saying' of set prayers such as the Lord's Prayer (Paternoster). As beginners proceed along this way, they may also engage in works of charity.

In order to undertake such reading, meditation, study,

---

[64] Anon, *The Cloud of Unknowing* [ed. Walsh], ch.35
[65] Walter [of] Hilton *The Scale of Perfection*, bk 1, ch.4

prayer and good works with due concentration and devotion, considerable self-discipline is required. Ignatius therefore commends the practices of fasting and flagellation. (The latter is an element of Ignatian spirituality normally overlooked today!) A more recent equivalent is the advice of Kenneth Leech: 'Before true prayer can begin, there must be a discipline of thought through the practice of silence and withdrawal, and a discipline of the body through the practice of some degree of physical solitude and stillness.'[66] Apart from acting as aids to acquiring the knowledge and love of God, such practices are designed to assist beginners in evaluating their own lives.

The first step is particularly concerned with a growing awareness of one's own sinfulness. So, for example, during the First Week of Ignatius' *Spiritual Exercises*, the beginner is urged to examine his or her life in detail in order to become aware of past sins and the need for change and growth. Usually this results in both a need and a desire to confess one's sins and see the very foundations of one's life reformed. Ignatius assumes that confession will be formal, before a priest, but Hilton, the *Cloud* and others also encourage private confession before God;

> 'God's Word, whether written or spoken, is like a mirror ... it follows, then, that when a person sees in the bodily or spiritual mirror ... just where the dirty mark is on his bodily or spiritual face, he goes to the well to wash it off – and not before. Now if this mark is a particular sin, the well is holy church and the water confession, with all its elements. And if the mark is simply the blind root with the impulse to sin, then the well is the merciful God, and the water is prayer,

---

[66] K. Leech *Soul Friend: A Study of Spirituality*, Sheldon Press, 1977, p.179; the 'discipline of thought' is sometimes called 'recollection'.

with all its elements.'[67]

Thus the way of purgation seeks to establish a more authentic evaluation of the self, and a more truthful relationship with God, encouraging openness and honesty before Him. Negatively, it is a renunciation of 'worldly' behaviour, habits, thoughts, attachments and attitudes.

(ii) *The way of illumination, also known as 'the state of proficients', during which the soul is illuminated by the pure 'light' (= the loving grace) of God. In contrast to the busy activity of the way of purgation, this takes place in the quiet prayer of contemplation.*

John of the Cross explains:

> 'When this house of the senses was stilled (that is, mortified), its passions quenched, and its appetites calmed and put to sleep through this happy night of the purgation of the sense, the soul went out in order to begin its journey along the road of the spirit, which is that of Proficients and which by another terminology is referred to as the illuminative way or the way of infused contemplation.'[68]

> 'The ... surest sign is that a person likes to remain alone in loving awareness of God, without particular considerations, in interior peace and quiet and repose.'[69]

In other words, entry to this second stage is marked by a shift from activity to stillness, from discursive prayer to a more contemplative and extempore form of prayer. It is also characterised by a heightened sense of God's loving

---

[67] Anon, *The Cloud of Unknowing*, ch.35
[68] John of the Cross *The Dark Night of The Soul* in *The Complete Works*, I.14.I
[69] John of the Cross *The Ascent of Mount Carmel* in *The Complete Works*, 2.13.2-4

goodness, no more illusions about one's own goodness, and a great feeling of love for God.

For Hilton, for example,

> 'The second part of contemplation lies principally in affection ... Sometimes a man or woman meditating on God feels a fervour of love and spiritual sweetness in the remembrance of his passion, or any of his works in his humanity; or he feels great trust in the goodness and mercy of God for the forgiveness of sins, and for his gifts of grace ... He cannot explain what it is, but he feels it plainly ... making him feel that he does not care what then becomes of him provided the will of God is fulfilled.'[70]

Later on the illuminative way, the proficient comes to what John calls 'the dark night of the soul' – the most intense experience of this way, and its culminating point. *The Cloud of Unknowing* advises, 'Do not hang back then, but labour in it until you experience the desire. For when you first begin to undertake it, all that you find is a darkness, a sort of cloud of unknowing, you cannot tell what it is, except that you experience in your will a simple reaching out to God.'[71]

The 'light' of God is now illuminating the proficient to such an extent that he or she feels completely unworthy and unable to sense his presence. This is a 'journey into the unknown', and there is much uncertainty, confusion and doubt. The proficient can make no sense of what is happening, and is keenly aware of his total dependence on God. John of the Cross calls this the 'state of spiritual betrothal'. Following the 'dark night of the soul', the 'spiritual pilgrim' enters ...

---

[70] Walter [of] Hilton, *The Scale of Perfection*, bk.1 ch.5
[71] Anon, *The Cloud of Unknowing*, ch.3

(iii)   *The way of union, also known as the 'state of perfection', during which the mystic approaches the goal of the spiritual mystical 'journey', variously called union or perfection or 'fullness of life'.*

John of the Cross explains that, where proficients may experience some sense of God's presence ('touches of union'), with 'perfects' a substantial union with God is established, and they habitually experience his presence,[72] enjoying a 'sweetness and tranquillity that is never lost or lacking'.[73] John calls this 'the state of spiritual marriage'.

'This spiritual marriage', he writes, 'is incomparably greater than the spiritual betrothal, for it is a total transformation in the Beloved, in which each surrenders the entire possession of self to the other with a certain consummation of the union of love. The soul thereby becomes divine, God through participation, insofar as is possible in this life. ... It is accordingly the highest state attainable in this life.'[74] Strangely, though, John asserts that, even in this highest of all states, 'love can grow deeper in quality ... and become more ardent.'[75]

Contemplation has now grown to become 'simple loving attention to the presence of God'; prayer has become wordless adoration. According to Teresa of Avila, if genuine, this will be verified by practical service of some kind. Service which is guaranteed to be effective, for, where the beginner and the proficient knew God through his creation, the

---

[72] John of the Cross, *The Spiritual Canticle* in *The Complete Works*, stanzas 20, 21:12-13; 2.5
[73] ibid, stanza 24.5
[74] ibid, stanza 22.3
[75] John of the Cross *The Living Flame of Love*, in *The Complete Works*, Prologue 3

'perfect' knows the creation through its God, because he shares God's perspective on all things. And powerful service, for the 'perfect' has immediate access to all the abundance of grace. Ignatius is generally regarded as a good example of this mystical ideal of being at once contemplative and active. Underhill remarks that this stage 'brings astonishing access of energy and endurance, a power of dealing with persons and events far beyond the self's natural capacities.'[76]

Teresa says of this final union: 'I can only say that the Lord wishes to reveal for that moment ... the glory of heaven.'[77] John describes the summit of the mountain as 'the high state of perfection.'[78] Walter Hilton sums it up thus:

'... as perfect as can be here, [it] lies both in cognition and in affection; that is to say, in the knowing and perfect loving of God. That is when a person's soul is first cleansed from all sins and reformed to the image of Jesus by completeness of virtues, and afterward he is visited and taken up from all earthly and fleshly affections ... and then is illumined by the grace of the Holy Spirit to see intellectually the Truth, which is God, and also spiritual things, with a soft, sweet, burning love for him.'[79]

Incredibly, by this stage, temptation and sin have almost ceased to exist (!) A 'perfect' is still capable of falling into sin, but is unlikely to do so because the attraction to sin no longer has a compelling hold. 'Old lovers hardly ever fail God, for they now stand above all that would make them fail him.'[80]

---

[76] E. Underhill, *Mystics of the Church*, Cambridge: Clarke, 1925, p.27
[77] Teresa of Avila, *The Interior Castle*, op. cit., p.178
[78] John of the Cross, *The Ascent of Mount Carmel*, in *The Complete Works*, I.II.I
[79] Walter [of] Hilton, *The Scale of Perfection*, Bk 1 ch.8
[80] John of the Cross, *The Spiritual Canticle* in *The Complete Works*, stanza

Such statements have laid many of the classic mystics (John of the Cross, in particular) wide open to charges of perfectionism, for, as Burrows comments 'there is no ego on the summit of the mountain.'[81]

For the English mystics, the state of union with God was available to anyone who would take the 'threefold way'; but for most of the continental mystics, union was something granted by God only to a chosen few. Brother Lawrence, for example, writes, 'Only a few persons attain this state; it is a grace which God bestows on certain chosen souls.'[82] And Teresa misquotes Matthew 22:14, 'many are called but few are chosen.'[83]

Some of the mystics add a fourth stage, to be enjoyed either only or chiefly in heaven. Thereby they largely avoid the charges of perfectionism levelled at 'three-stagers' like John of the Cross. 'My spiritual friend in God, you are to understand that ... there are four degrees and forms of the Christian life ... Three of these can be begun and ended in this life, and one may begin the fourth by grace here below, which is to last without end in the happiness of heaven.'[84]

The Spanish mystics, however, all make explicit use of the threefold way in their writings. John himself focuses on the way of purgation in *The Dark Night of the Soul* and *The Ascent of Mount Carmel*, and on the ways of illumination and union in *The Spiritual Canticle* and *The Living Flame of*

25:11

[81] R. Burrows *Ascent to Love: The Spiritual Teaching of St John of the Cross*, London: DLT, 1987, p.115

[82] Brother Lawrence *The Practice of the Presence of God*, p.126

[83] Teresa of Avila, *The Interior Castle*, 5.1.2, p.85

[84] Anon, *The Cloud of Unknowing*, ch.1; Walter [of] Hilton's programme also has four stages.

Love. In Teresa's *Interior Castle*, the first few 'dwelling places' relate to the way of purification, the middle ones to the way of illumination, and the last three to the way of union, with spiritual marriage taking place in the seventh 'dwelling place'. Ignatius relates the First Week of his *Spiritual Exercises* to the way of purification, while weeks two and three correspond to the way of illumination. With some of the English mystics, (e.g. Julian) the threefold structure is less clear, but distinguishing characteristics of the three stages are still detectable.

Needless to say, there is little basis for 'the threefold way' in scripture. As McGinn admits one cannot find explicit mysticism in the Bible to match the sense in which Origen or Bernard of Clairvaux or Pseudo-Dionysius or Julian or John of the Cross wrote of it.[85]

In the Middle Ages there was some debate over whether or not these three (or four) stages were always experienced successively. The Franciscans decided they need not be strictly temporal, and most modern mystics would (at least in theory) agree. The 'three ways' are therefore sometimes described as 'cyclical movements of grace', the characteristics of the stages being present in different proportions at points all along the 'spiritual journey'. However, we have to say that most presentations of the 'threefold way' still read as if 'progress' is strictly temporal and successive, an impression reinforced by the habit of calling the stages those of 'the beginners, the proficient and the perfect'.

The 'threefold way' as a model for spiritual growth is

---

[85] B. McGinn, in *The New SCM Dictionary of Christian Spirituality*, op. cit., p.19

still widely accepted today. There have been very few challenges to it from beyond evangelicalism (and not enough within!). The key exception is the Jesuit mystic Karl Rahner. He challenges the concept of thinking of the spiritual life in terms of distinct stages as based on an outdated neoplatonic anthropology.[86] But for the most part, among liberals and Catholics, the threefold way is simply assumed. Ordinands study it in Catholic and Anglo-Catholic seminaries in order to be able to guide 'persons seeking perfection' in the confessional and beyond. With that aim in mind, many have tried to integrate it with modern psychological understandings of spiritual development.[87] As a result probably the majority of non-evangelicals[88] believe that doubt and uncertainty are both necessary and essential for spiritual growth; that people *need* to question all their previously held beliefs and, paradoxically, go through an 'unknowing', a spiritual 'darkness', in order to reach 'maturity'.

Furthermore, if the three stages of the mystical way are regarded as successive (as in practice they usually are), then, for many, 'progress' through them involves leaving such activities as scripture reading and verbal prayer behind. Such practices are characteristic of the way of purgation, which is not generally expected to last very long. (The way of illumination, by contrast, may last many years). Therefore many non-evangelicals also believe that a devotional life such as the traditional evangelical Quiet Time, consisting of little but scripture reading, reflection and verbal prayer, is the practice of an immature Christian – still on the first rungs of

---

[86] In K. Rahner *The Theological Investigations 3*, London: DLT, 1967
[87] For example, James Fowler in *Faithful Change* Nashville: Abingdon, 1996
[88] For example, the ever popular Kenneth Leech, in *Soul Friend*.

the ladder, in the 'state of beginners'. People are expected, and encouraged, to grow out of this 'elementary' stage; to grow beyond it in the direction of wordless contemplation.[89]

In fact, of course, it is precisely those devotions not centred on the Word of God and biblical prayer which develop immature Christians. The desire to set out on 'the threefold way' may come from an admirable recognition of the need for spiritual growth, but there are serious problems with the model of spiritual growth it presupposes. For convenience, these may be broadly divided into two groups.[90] First,

5.   The problems of Greek Philosophy

'Christian mysticism' in general, and the 'threefold way' in particular, are the product of a marriage between essentially pre-Reformation Christianity and neoplatonism, and its mixed parentage is still all too evident.

Neoplatonism was developed from Platonism chiefly by the philosopher Plotinus (205-270 AD). It had three key features which subsequently influenced the development of 'Christian mysticism': a radical material / spiritual dualism, a belief in 'progress' by contemplation, and the goal of union with the platonic 'One', that 'absolute reality' which Plotinus called 'God'.

---

[89] See, for example, F.P. Harton in *The Elements of the Spiritual Life* London: SPCK, 1932
[90] My division is somewhat arbitrary because neoplatonism has considerably influenced Catholic theology.

5.1. *The problem of dualism: it devalues creation*

From Plato, Plotinus inherited the belief in a fundamental dualism between the physical, material world and the spiritual world, between the human soul and the human body. The material world was the realm of imperfection, transience and illusion; the spiritual world was the realm of perfection and permanence. The human soul's purpose in life was to detach itself from all that was 'worldly', including the material body in which it was 'imprisoned', and ascend to the spiritual world where it truly belonged. (This philosophy has affected us more than we realise. Christians today often speak in neoplatonic terms, e.g. of 'the soul's immortality', or the body being 'just a shell', as if soul and body were readily separable, and the latter of no eternal consequence.)

Detachment from the physical world was by means of a strict, ascetic self-discipline. The same sort of self-discipline, with the same intention, typically characterises the first stage of 'the threefold way', the 'way of purgation.' So John Climacus writes, 'Detachment from the things perceived by the senses means the vision of things spiritual.'[91] Similarly, Hilton speaks of the soul being 'as if forcibly ravished out of the bodily sense.'[92] And John of the Cross says 'a soul must strip itself of all creatures and of its actions and abilities so that, when everything unlike and unconformed to God is cast out, it may receive the likeness of God.'[93]

Associated with detachment is mortification of the body, a deliberate 'killing' of one's own passions. John Climacus again: 'Treat your body always as an enemy, for

---

[91] John Climacus, *The Ladder of Divine Ascent*, p.256
[92] Walter [of] Hilton, *The Scale of Perfection*, bk 1 ch.8
[93] John of the Cross, *The Ascent of Mount Carmel*, 2.5.4

flesh is an ungrateful and treacherous friend.'[94] And John of the Cross: 'The road and ascent to God, then, necessarily demands a habitual effort to renounce and mortify the appetites; the sooner this mortification is achieved, the sooner the soul reaches the top.'[95] More recently, Miles described the method of ascent as the 'renunciation of all earthly things,'[96] and Underhill insisted that 'the ascetic foundation, in one form or another, is the only enduring foundation of a sane, contemplative life.'[97]

What will be a genuinely evangelical response to such an asceticism? Positively, we can of course welcome a right seriousness with regard to sin. A healthy sense of sin is an essential precursor to real repentance, faith in Christ, forgiveness, and, thereby, salvation. A healthy sense of sin is, therefore, one ingredient of a truly Christian spirituality. Furthermore, there is a right place for self-denial and self-discipline in the Christian life, for 'training ourselves in godliness'.[98]

However, to view the entire material world, including the mind and body, as an inevitable hindrance to spiritual progress is to devalue the physical creation in a way that runs directly counter to biblical teaching.[99] Such a negative attitude toward the body and the world is more neoplatonic

---

[94] John Climacus, *The Ladder of Divine Ascent*, p.153
[95] John of the Cross *The Ascent of Mount Carmel*, 1.5.6
[96] M.R. Miles, *The Image and Practice of Holiness*, London:SCM, 1988, p.66
[97] E. Underhill, *Practical Mysticism*, p.42
[98] See, for example, Mark 8:34, 1 Timothy 4:7f, 2 Timothy 1:7, Hebrews 12:11f.
[99] See, for example Genesis 1:31, 1 Corinthians 15:35ff, Colossians 2:20-23, 1 Timothy 4:4

than biblical. As John Pearce points out, Christians 'are not seeking to escape from the body into some 'higher state' ... We need to remember that the Bible ... is fundamentally world-affirming not world-denying.'[100]

5.2. The problem of contemplation: it redefines prayer

For neoplatonists, contemplation (Greek: *theoria*) was the means by which the soul progressed, bringing it ever closer to God until finally union was achieved.

The mystics 'Christianised' this concept, equating contemplation, or at least the practical expression of contemplation, with the highest form of prayer. For them, each of the stages of the mystical way was associated with a particular kind of prayer. 'You are to understand that there are three kinds of prayer. The first is spoken prayer,'[101] by which they meant verbal prayer in set liturgical forms such as would be found in Mattins, Vespers or Compline. Teresa says of this kind of prayer, '[it] is a weary effort with small returns; the well may run dry.'[102] It was simply the foundation for all other forms of prayer.

The second degree of prayer 'is spoken, but without any particular set words, and this is when a man or woman feels the grace of devotion by the gift of God, and in his devotion speaks to him as if he were bodily in his presence.'[103] In the light of its context, such encouragement to extempore personal prayer is refreshing.

---

[100] J.F.D. Pearce, A Critique of Spirituality, Oxford: Latimer study no. 52, pp.11,14
[101] W. Hilton, The Scale of Perfection, bk1, ch.26f
[102] Teresa of Avila The Life of Saint Teresa chs 11-19, Penguin, 1957, p.78ff
[103] ibid., bk 1, ch.29

The third degree of prayer is silent, largely wordless, contemplation.[104] At its heart, contemplation is a simple sensing and enjoyment of God's loving presence. 'In my prayer I was reaching out to heaven with heartfelt longing when I became aware, in a way I cannot explain, of a symphony of song, and in myself I sensed a corresponding harmony at once wholly delectable and heavenly, which persisted in my mind.'[105] Of this kind of prayer, Teresa writes, '[It] cannot be described in words ... there is no more toil and the seasons no longer change ... The soul enjoys undoubting certitude; the faculties work without effort and without consciousness ...'[106]

Since, for the apophatic mystic, God is essentially unknowable and inexpressible, it is appropriate to approach him with silence. If words are used, they are few and much repeated, for example, 'Lord, have mercy'. But, for the most part, words are regarded as at best unnecessary, at worst positive obstacles to union. Alison Fry comments: 'wordless adoration is the closest we come to praying continually'.[107] Contemplative prayer is thus seen as a 'higher', more intimate form of prayer than that which uses words.

Most mystics further recognise, following Evagrius and the Desert Fathers, that the silence necessary for a contemplative life is best maintained in solitude.

> 'Whoever has this gift of God fervently needs to escape for the time from the presence and company of everyone, and

---

[104] Not to be confused with the more cerebral and object or scripture-focused 'meditation.'
[105] R. Rolle, *The Fire of Love*, ch.15
[106] Teresa of Avila *The Life of Saint Teresa*, p.78ff
[107] Alison Fry, *Learning from the English Mystics*, p.19f

to be alone, lest he should be hindered."[108]

This line of thought is sometimes extended to promote solitude as the best context, not only for prayer, but for spiritual growth generally. Henri Nouwen has argued that Christians need to create their own, inner 'desert', for solitude is 'the place where the emergence of the new man and the new woman occurs,'[109] and David Runcorn similarly maintains that in solitude 'life is renewed, restored and given its true perspective.'[110]

Many claim biblical support for these views in texts like 'Be still and know that I am God' and Elijah's experience of the 'still, small voice'.[111] A greater attention to context might lead them to realise that Psalm 46:10 is not a call to mystic silence but to trust in Almighty God, and that Elijah was not wisely retreating to hear God's unspoken voice in solitude but fleeing from Jezebel in fear and panic. In fact, as Mike Raiter points out, what finally effected 'spiritual growth' in his life was not the experience of silence but the spoken word of God which followed it.[112]

Evangelicals, of course, would not wish to deny that solitude and silence can be conducive to spiritual growth, or at least to spiritual health. Even Jesus opted for solitude occasionally! We agree, with Fry, that some solitude may force us to 'face our own state before God, and so allow God

---

[108] Walter [of] Hilton, *The Scale of Perfection*, bk 1, ch.30
[109] H. Nouwen, *The Way of The Heart: Desert Spirituality and Contemporary Ministry* London: DLT, 1981 p.27
[110] D. Runcorn, *Space for God* London: Daybreak, 1990, p.7
[111] Psalm 46:10 and 1 Kings 19:12 (NRSV: 'a sound of sheer silence') respectively.
[112] 1 Kings 19:13-18; see M. Raiter *Stirrings of the Soul*, p.178

to deal with us.'[113]   Nevertheless we must not turn such valuable 'times alone with God' into a general life-controlling rule for all Christians always. We must not denigrate words and company when we worship a Triune God who chose to reveal himself in words and to call out for himself not just one individual but a whole people. For the Bible teaches that God and his will are revealed in his word, not in silence, and that the primary and proper context for 'spiritual growth' is community, not solitude.'[114]

In medieval times, the contemplative or mystical life (of solitary withdrawal) was distinguished from the active life (in the world). The latter involved a deliberate, outward, pursuit of good works; the former involved a deliberate, inward detachment from earthly things and absorption with God and spiritual things. Most mystics regarded the contemplative life as superior, citing Mary as the classic biblical example of one who chose 'the better portion' of simple, quiet, loving, 'being' in Jesus' presence, in contrast to the more active Martha.'[115] Walter Hilton was an exception; he wrote *The Mixed Life* specifically to encourage Christians, 'sometimes to use the works of mercy in active life ... and sometimes for to leave all manner of outward business, and give themselves unto prayers and meditations, reading of Holy Writ, and to other ghostly occupations.'[116] Most modern writers would agree with Hilton: 'In reality the active and contemplative paths cannot be entirely separated.'[117] One consequence of this is that, though contemplation has

---

[113] Alison Fry, *Learning from the English Mystics*, p.15
[114] 2 Timothy 3:16; Colossians 3:1-17; Ephesians 4:7-16; 1 Peter 2
[115] Luke 10:42; see e.g. *The Cloud of Unknowing*, ch.21
[116] Walter [of] Hilton, *The Mixed Life*, ch.5
[117] Alison Fry, *Learning from the English Mystics*, p.12

traditionally been viewed as the special 'grace-gift' of the mystic, more recently, techniques such as 'centering' have been used to help 'ordinary Christians' engage in this 'highest form' of prayer.

The Cloud of Unknowing defines prayer as 'nothing but a devout reaching out directly to God,'[118] but that is not the Bible's definition of prayer. As John Owen says, 'whatever there may be in the height of 'contemplative prayer' as it is called, it neither is prayer nor can any account be so esteemed.'[119] Biblically, prayer is not primarily about sensing and enjoying God's presence. Rather, following Raiter, 'the essence of prayer is petition.'[120] I would add, 'in a context of praise and/or thanksgiving.'[121] And its purpose is not to experience God, but to see our wills conformed to his. Mysticism, by contrast, sees petition as the lowest form of prayer, largely because it is so word-dependent. It is entirely wrong so to devalue words. After all, from the very beginning, God has revealed himself as a God who speaks, who makes himself known through words, and who has made us in his image as beings who communicate through words. Cyprian (the 3rd century bishop of Carthage) rightly said: 'in prayer you speak to God, in reading God speaks to you.' It is precisely in petition-with-thanksgiving that we most recognise our complete dependence on our Creator. Evangelicals are therefore right to regard so-called 'higher forms' of prayer with suspicion and extreme caution.

---

[118] Anon, *The Cloud of Unknowing*, ch.39
[119] John Owen, *The Work of the Holy Spirit in Prayer*, orig. pubd. 1682; in *The Works of John Owen* [ed. Gould], vol 4, Edinburgh: Banner of Truth Trust, 1967, p.334f
[120] M. Raiter, *Stirrings of the Soul*, p.180
[121] See, for example, Matthew 6:7-13, 7:7-11, Luke18:1-8, Philippians 4:6

5.3. The problem of union: the 'mystical way' ends where it should begin

Mysticism sees union with God as the goal of spirituality. Bonaventure portrayed this union as a coming to share in the intra-trinitarian knowing and loving of the divine persons.[122] John of the Cross portrayed it as 'spiritual marriage', and one of its key characteristics was ecstatic joy.

Recently, some have argued that 'a broad and flexible understanding of mysticism need not take the language of union with God as the defining characteristic.'[123] Nonetheless, most of the classic mystical writers and many contemporary ones do so take it. They see union with God as the endpoint of spiritual growth where the Bible sees union with God (in Christ) as the starting point and prerequisite for spiritual growth.[124] For scripture is quite clear: growing to maturity as a Christian has nothing whatever to do with our being drawn into an ever closer union with God.[125] Rather, Christians are united to Christ from the very moment of conversion.[126] The Israelites may have had to ascend Mount Zion to reach and enjoy God's presence (Psalms 120-134), but we 'have come to Mount Zion, and to the city of the living God, the heavenly Jerusalem.'[127] The tense of the verb ('have come') is perfect; it speaks of an action completed in the past

---

[122] In *The Journey of the Mind into God*, ch.VI
[123] B. McGinn 'The Nature of Mysticism' in *The New SCM Dictionary of Christian Spirituality*, p.19
[124] As Philip Sheldrake rightly points out in an article on 'Journey, Spiritual' in *The New SCM Dictionary of Christian Spirituality*, p.389
[125] See, for example, Ephesians 4:13f; Philippians 3:14f; Hebrews 5:14; James 3:2
[126] See, for example, Romans 6:5; 2 Corinthians 13:5; Galatians 2:20; Colossians 2:10, 18f
[127] Hebrews 12:22

but with ongoing effects.

Because of Christ's finished work in his death, resurrection and ascension, we may freely experience all the joy of his presence without having to climb any ladders or mountains.[128] He has raised us up to live permanently with him 'in the heavenly places'. Paul uses the telling phrase 'in Christ' to express this fact. He makes it clear that we cannot achieve any greater union with God than he has already achieved for us and in which, by grace, we daily stand. Instead, spiritual growth is about an ever-increasing conformity to the Christ with whom we are united. It is about our union with Him growing ever richer, not ever closer.[129] Ferguson measuredly comments, 'It is insufficiently stressed [by contemplatives] that what [Christ] has done actually gives us access to God.'[130] In theological language, mystics have an under-realized eschatology (surprisingly, considering the charges of perfectionism).

6.   The problems of Roman Catholic theology

Many of the classic mystics were reacting in various ways against the Roman Catholicism of their day: Richard Rolle, for example, in *The Fire of Love*, reacted against asceticism, believing that what mattered most was a passionate, loving commitment to God.   He wrote scathingly about clerics

---

[128] See, for example, Hebrews 4:14-16; Ephesians 2:18f

[129] Again, this is more fully developed in my own *Presenting Everyone Mature.*

[130] S.B. Ferguson, 'A Reformed Response' [to the contemplative view of sanctification] in *Christian Spirituality: Five Views of Sanctification*, Illinois: IVP, 1988, p.194

'whom he felt knew nothing of the love of God.'[131]   Ignatius, too, longed to see Christians much more Christ-centred. Both obviously had a high regard for scripture, and their works are full of biblical quotations. Sadly, neither they nor any of the other 'classic' mystics were equipped to handle scripture well. As a result, their 'reactions' are simply not radical enough, and their fundamental Catholicism still betrays itself. For example, Rolle still happily speaks of purgatory, and Ignatius of penances and prayers to Mary. More importantly, for our present considerations, they all simply assume an essentially Catholic model of spiritual growth. This has a number of key problems (still evident in modern Catholicism).

6.1.   The problem of starting with baptism: it fails to identify the unconverted

For Catholics, spiritual growth begins with the 'infusion' of divine grace at baptism (which functions *ex opere operato*). The 'classic' mystics all lived in times when virtually everyone around them was baptised. Therefore, it's not surprising that they all simply assume in their writings that both they and their readers are already Christians – an assumption which is not always quite so self-evident to us! Indeed, some of the experiences the mystics describe along their 'mystical way' resonate far more with our evangelical understanding of pre-conversion.

Take John of the Cross's 'dark night of the soul', for example, with all its doubts and feelings of distance from God. Before I was converted, I remember feeling that my prayers 'weren't getting through'; I felt as if there were a big,

---

[131] Alison Fry, *Learning from the English Mystics*, op. cit., p.5

black cloud between me and God. I was right, of course; the cloud was called 'my sin', and at that time it had yet to be dealt with. Maybe John and others are really reflecting the experiences of those we would identify as 'genuine seekers'.

There is much support for this theory in the texts themselves, especially in the growing awareness of personal sin. For example:

> '... take good, gracious God just as he is, and without further ado lay him on your sick self just as you are, for all the world as if he were a poultice! Or to put it in other words, lift up your sick self just as you are, and through your longing strive to touch good, gracious God just as He is. Touching him who is eternal health, which is the point of the story of the woman in the gospel who said, '... If I touch but the hem of his garment, I shall be whole ...'"[132]

Does that not read primarily as advice to the as-yet-unconverted? Tellingly, many writers on mysticism unwittingly draw a similar conclusion. Thus, Alison Fry says of the English mystics, 'they acted as helpers and guides to faithful people who were sincerely seeking God ...'[133]

Certainly, if many of those who took the 'mystical way' were in fact unconverted (and therefore did not know God personally), that would explain many things. It would explain why some distinguish Bible reading and study as a way of knowing *about* God from the mystical life as a way of knowing God intimately. Perhaps most significant of all, it would explain much of the development of 'negative' mystical theology. It was Pseudo-Dionysius who first used the term 'mystical theology', circa 500AD, to indicate 'knowledge' of

---

[132] Anon, *Epistle of Privy Counsel*, ch.2
[133] Alison Fry, *Learning from the English Mystics*, p.4

45

the God who is essentially indescribable and unknowable. Based on this doctrine of the 'unknowability' of God, an apophatic spirituality developed which reached a climax in the works of John of the Cross. To John, God 'is dark night to the soul in this life', hence 'the soul has to proceed rather by unknowing than by knowing' and must eventually pass 'beyond everything to unknowing'.[134] Such views now find new expression in contemporary writings such as those of Kenneth Leech[135] or Rowan Williams.[136]

Following Pseudo-Dionysius and John of the Cross, some mystics have been inclined to turn reasonable assertions that we cannot fully know God into unbiblical assertions that we cannot truly know him at all. Inevitably, many also downplay the role of the mind and the physical senses in relating to God. For Pseudo-Dionysius, in the presence of God, the mind 'will turn silent completely, since it will finally be at one with him who is indescribable.'[137] John of the Cross warns, 'Great, therefore, is the error of many ... who have practiced approaching God by means of images and forms and meditations as befits beginners.'[138] *The Cloud of Unknowing's* insistence that God can only be known by love, not reason,[139] is often taken today as anti-intellectualism. And, more recently, Underhill speaks of 'human consciousness'

---

[134] John of the Cross, *The Ascent of Mount Carmel*, in *The Complete Works*, 1:4
[135] e.g. K. Leech *Soul Friend: A Study of Spirituality.*
[136] e.g. R. Williams *The Wound of Knowledge*, DLT, revised edition 1990, ch.8
[137] Dionysius, *Mystical Theology 3*
[138] John of the Cross, *The Ascent of Mount Carmel*, in *The Complete Works*, p.112
[139] Anon, *The Cloud of Unknowing*, ch.4

ascending 'from thought to contemplation',[140] and Muto comments that we must live 'in formative detachment or sensory deprivation ... we must ... be able to suspend rational categories.'[141]

Clearly evangelicals need to tread very warily here, for as Raiter rightly notes, this 'cuts right across the glorious, liberating news of the gospel.'[142] After all, the gospel message demands that God *is* knowable, and has freely chosen to be so. What's more, the scriptures tell us that his revelation of himself, though not complete, is both adequate and fully reliable. 'In Christ', we can know God truly without knowing him fully.[143] Furthermore, scripture does not downplay the role of the human mind in spiritual growth. Paul does explain that an *unaided* human mind is incapable of 'knowing God'; that such relational knowledge comes only by means of the Spirit of God working with and through the Word of God to bring us into union with Christ and *his* mind. Nonetheless, it is precisely as we apply our converted, 'renewed' minds to understanding and applying scripture that we grow spiritually, not by leaving our minds behind.[144]

Bonaventure was right to emphasise that Christians share in the intra-trinitarian knowing and loving of the three persons of the Godhead, but that union is not attained by means of some post-baptismal 'mystical journey into God'; rather, by grace through repentance and faith we share in

---

[140] E. Underhill, *Practical Mysticism*, p.12
[141] S.A. Muto, *John of the Cross for Today*, Indiana: Ave Maria Press, p.42
[142] M. Raiter, *Stirrings of the Soul*, p.162
[143] See, for example: John 1:18; John 14:6f; John 17:3, 25f; Acts 17:23; 1 John 5:20.
[144] See, for example: 1 Corinthians 2:11-16; Ephesians 1:17-19; 2 Timothy 3:16f

such knowing and loving from the very moment of conversion.[145] Which brings us to the second key problem of mysticism's Roman Catholic theological foundation.

6.2. The problem of under-emphasising grace: it undermines assurance

Evangelicals have traditionally accused mysticism of endorsing salvation 'by works'. Anders Nygren, for example: 'Its main preoccupation is with man's way to God. It is essentially self-salvation by means of an ascent to the Divine.'[146] When confronted with this charge, the mystics will strongly deny it, many of them insisting that the mystical experience is all of grace. Of the 'classics', both John and Teresa view contemplation as a gift of grace; they see it primarily, not as the work of the human soul, but as God's work within the human soul. Similarly, as noted earlier, most recent writers on mysticism are eager to point out that the mystical experience itself is essentially something which happens *to* the mystic, not something which he or she can initiate. 'The mystics could teach contemplation, but only God could give the 'mystical' experience of union with himself.'[147]

However, one has to say that, if the priority of grace is believed, it is certainly not made sufficiently clear, either in the classic texts or in the modern ones. Therefore in practice the impression received is one of the priority of works and effort. Consider the following extracts:

Teresa of Avila:

---

[145] Ephesians 2:8
[146] A. Nygren, *Eros and Agape*, [trans Watson] London, SPCK, 1953, p.220f
[147] Alison Fry, *Learning from the English Mystics*, p.11f

48

'True union can very well be reached, with God's help, if we make the effort to obtain it by keeping our wills fixed only on that which is God's will.'[148]

The *Cloud of Unknowing*:

'Lift up your heart to God ... loathe to think on aught but himself. ... Do your best to forget all the creatures that ever God made and their works. ... This is the work of the soul that most pleases God. ... Cease not, therefore, but travail until you feel longing ...'[149]

'Prayer in itself is nothing but a devout reaching out directly to God, in order to attain the good and to do away with evil.'[150]

Brother Lawrence:

'The shortest way to come to God was by a continual exercise of love, doing all things for his sake'[151]

'By ... unceasing turning to God we shall crush the head of Satan and strike his weapons from our hands.'[152]

The apparent contradiction is partly due to a peculiarly Catholic concept of grace.[153]

Catholics believe there are different kinds of grace. Of particular importance for our purposes are:

(i)   prevenient sanctifying grace, which is infused at baptism (*ex opere operato*), enabling the Catholic to

---

[148] Teresa of Avila, *The Interior Castle*, p.98
[149] Anon, *The Cloud of Unknowing*, ch.3
[150] ibid., ch.39
[151] Brother Lawrence *The Practice of the Presence of God*, 2nd conversation, p.39f
[152] ibid., p.111
[153] the Roman and Anglo-Catholic concept of grace is also distinctive in that grace seems to be regarded as almost a measurable 'substance'.

believe (i.e. assent to doctrine as contained in the catholic creeds), and thus be justified. From then on, the baptised person is described as in a 'state of grace', and is commanded to preserve that state. Sanctifying grace also infuses into the soul the virtues of faith, hope and charity/love. 'These virtues are not acquired by any human effort so that even baptised infants possess the infused virtues.'[154]

(ii)   efficacious grace, which operates post-baptism, by cooperation with the will, enabling the individual to seek Christ, avoid sin, obey God and do good.

Thus the baptised young Catholic is advised: 'As a Catholic you are called to seek and find Christ. But you did not begin this quest on your own initiative. The initiative was all God's. ... God first found you and made you visibly his in baptism. What he seeks now is that you seek Him. In a mysterious way your whole life with God is an ongoing quest for each other by two lovers – God and you – who already possess each other.'[155] Thus grace (infused, sanctifying) can always be said to have priority because it dates back to baptism, but in the practice of everyday living and growing, grace (efficacious) meets effort half way. Hardly the same sort of 'priority' as the Reformers' *sola gratia*.

The consequences of this understanding of grace for mystics are predictable: they characteristically lack any solid assurance of salvation. When Brother Lawrence anticipates his own death, for example, he expects to experience purgatory and admits he is uncertain about his own future.

---

[154] *The Essential Catholic Handbook*, [ed. S. Finnegan] Canterbury Press, 1997, p.193
[155] ibid., p4, quoting *Catechism of the Catholic Church* 50-53, 521

'Whether I am lost or saved, I want simply to go on living entirely for God.'[156] But perhaps the lack of assurance is most graphically demonstrated by the illustration which accompanied one version of John Climacus' *The Ladder of Divine Ascent*.[157] The picture shows Christians ascending the ladder to God. On the way, demons pull some off and pierce others with demonic arrows. As Miles comments, this imagery 'renders more dramatic the possibility of sudden collapse and precipitous descent ... into the gaping mouth of hell.'[158] Those who take the 'mystical way' to union with God know the possiblity of failure is very real. Not too surprising then, that mystical theology has been criticised 'on the grounds of its implicit neglect of attention to God's gracious and sustaining care for Christians.'[159]

6.3. The problem of authority: it's just not sola scriptura

We have to recognise that, in the context of their own time, many of the classic medieval mystics were generally orthodox and even doctrinally conservative.

There's no doubt that some, at least, were also people of genuine and devout faith. Think of Julian's longing to understand and share more of the sufferings of Christ, for example, or Ignatius' love for meditating on scripture. For the most part, it seems they *wanted* to be thoroughly biblical. Indeed, some at least obviously thought they *were* being thoroughly biblical, as evidenced by the fact that their works are liberally 'supported' with biblical quotations and

---

[156] Brother Lawrence *The Practice of the Presence of God*, p.35
[157] John Climacus, *The Ladder of Divine Ascent*, St. Catherine's Monastery, Sinai, frontispiece
[158] M.R. Miles, *The Image and Practice of Holiness*, p.66
[159] ibid., p.78

allusions, albeit frequently divorced from their original context.

However, their writings also make clear that scripture is not their sole authority. For a start, as good Catholics, the teaching of the church is at least equally authoritative (with the possible exception of Richard Rolle). We've already noticed that peculiarly Catholic doctrines and practices such as purgatory or praying to Mary are both commonplace and completely unchallenged. Teresa of Avila (keenly aware of the Inquisition!) prefaces *The Interior Castle* with this caveat:

> 'If I should say something that isn't in conformity with what the holy Roman Catholic church holds, it will be through ignorance and not through malice. This can be held as certain, and also that through the goodness of God I always am, and will be, and have been subject to her.'[160]

There is a third form of authority, too, at work behind these writings, for the mystics claim a 'higher' contemplative experience, involving direct contact with God. By this means, they say, they have received various forms of divine revelation. Julian of Norwich, for example, speaks of insight given her 'by bodily sight, by word formed in my understanding and by spiritual sight', and she clearly treats her visions of Christ's suffering and death as authoritative.[161] The *Cloud of Unknowing* explicitly teaches:

> God 'will perhaps, at some time, send out a beam of spiritual light that pierces the cloud of unknowing that is between you and him, and show you some of his secrets which no man may put into words.'[162]

---

[160] Teresa of Avila, *The Interior Castle*, prologue, p34
[161] Julian of Norwich, *Revelations of Divine Love*, First revelation, ch.9
[162] Anon, *The Cloud of Unknowing*, p70

As William James observed,

> 'Mystical states seem to those who experience them to be also states of knowledge ... They are illuminations, revelations ... and as a rule, they carry with them a curious sense of authority for after-time.'[163]

Therefore, while they would no doubt strongly deny it, in practice the mystics affirm another authority in addition to those of scripture and the church.

The results are inevitable. In some writings *(The Practice of the Presence of God, The Cloud of Unknowing)*, the Bible's focus on Jesus is almost completely missing. In some *(Revelations of Divine Love)*, there is clear doctrinal error or confusion,[164] and in others *(The Book of Margery Kempe)* the 'ascent' is into the realms of utter fantasy. The mystics show little awareness of the dangers of granting such authority to their own experiences. Teresa does explicitly admit that a mystic's visions could be delusions, and on a number of occasions 'sets down signs for discerning when there is deception.'[165] Unfortunately the test of scripture is not chief among them, and ultimately she remains confident in the mystic's own ability to discern the true from the false.

There is, of course, much more that could be said on the subject of mysticism. I have said nothing, for example, about the distinctive characteristics of Eastern mysticism, although it is in some spheres becoming more popular. Nor have I dealt with recent tendencies toward spiritual pluralism,

---

[163] W. James *The Varieties of Religious Experience*, p. 380
[164] Julian's obsession with God's 'love' leads her to reject both total depravity and his wrath as 'utterly impossible', and to speak of 'our precious mother Jesus'.
[165] For example, Teresa of Avila *The Interior Castle*, 5.1; 6.3, pp.85ff, 119ff

pragmatic individualism, and the 'hybridisation' of spiritualities, even though the growth of an eclectic spirituality rooted in practices rather than theology is a particularly 'slippery' new trend.

I think I should, however, say something about the recent trend among Protestants to revive the language of contemplative mysticism (which the Reformers rejected) and to argue for an evangelically acceptable version of mysticism. It may be that one could argue, as Corduan and Houston do, for the existence of such a 'biblical mysticism', but, as they both acknowledge, it would then amount to no more than 'the normal Christian life'. And that is not what evangelicals are taking on board when they read Ignatius or Julian, John of the Cross or Thomas Merton. Instead, they are encountering the threefold 'mystical way' with all its neoplatonic and Roman Catholic baggage. Only if mysticism could be entirely detached from an 'ascent to God' model of spiritual growth, and the threefold way in particular, could there be any possibility of it becoming acceptable to classic evangelicals, and that is most unlikely to happen! And, if it were to be so detached, and have no associations beyond the practice of normal biblical Christianity, then would it not be better to call it 'Christianity' anyway, and avoid all the inherent problems and dangers of the word 'mysticism'?

Evangelicals need more than ever to be discriminating, keeping a firm hold on the principle of submitting everything to the test of scripture. We must reaffirm, model and teach a thoroughly biblical model of spiritual growth and health. To that end, we do need to learn some lessons from the 'attractiveness' of mysticism. Maybe on occasion we have been 'too cerebral', too wary and belittling of experience and emotion. For the Word and the Spirit work together within whole persons to produce a genuine, deeply passionate and thoroughly experiential knowledge of the Lord. Furthermore, it is as we came to know Christ in the first place that we must go on and grow in him. It is as the Spirit continues to interpret the Word to us and apply it to our lives that we will grow to a healthy maturity, not by increasingly abandoning the Word in favour of the higher reaches of some mystical mountain or ladder.

As Peter warned the Christians of his day, 'Beware that you are not carried away ... and lose your own stability. But grow in the grace and knowledge of our Lord and Saviour Jesus Christ. To him be the glory both now and to the day of eternity. Amen.'[166]

7. Bibliography

Primary sources

Anon - *The Cloud of Unknowing* [ed. Walsh], Classics of Western Spirituality, New York: Paulist Press, 1981

Augustine - *The Confessions of St. Augustine* [trans. E.M. Blaicklock] Hodder & Stoughton, 1983

Bamberger, J. E. - *Evagrius Ponticus: Prakticos and Chapters on Prayer*, Cistercian Studies 4, Kalamazoo WI: Cistercian Publications, 1981

Benedict - *The Rule of Benedict*, [trans J. McCann] London: Sheed & Ward, 1976

Bonaventure - *Journey of the Mind into God* (*Itinerarium Mentis in Deum*), in *The Works of St. Bonaventure* [ed. P. Boehner & Z. Hayes] vol 2, revd ed., New York: Franciscan Institute Publications, 2002

Brother Lawrence [trans Attwater] *The Practice of the Presence of God*, Springfield: Templegate, 1974

Dionysius, *Mystical Theology 3* in *The Complete Works* [trans Luibheid] Classics of Western Spirituality London : SPCK, 1987

Edwards, Jonathan - *The Works of Jonathan Edwards* [ed. Goen], vol4, New Haven and London, 1972

Guigo II, *The Ladder of Monks II*; available at www.ldysinger.com

---

[166] 2 Peter 3:17f

Hilton, Walter [of] - *The Scale of Perfection* [ed. Clark & Dorwood], Classics of Western Spirituality, New York: Paulist Press, 1991

Hilton, Walter [of] - *The Mixed Life* in *The Minor Works of Walter Hilton* [ed. Jones], London: Burns & Oates & Washbourne, 1929

Ignatius of Loyola - G.E.Ganss et al [ed.] *Ignatius of Loyola: the Spiritual Exercises and selected works*, New York: Paulist Press, 1991

John Climacus, *The Ladder of Divine Ascent, Classics of Western Spirituality*, London: SPCK, 1982

John of the Cross - [trans / ed. Peers, E. Allison] *The Complete Works of St. John of the Cross*, London: Burns, Oates & Washbourne, 1947

Julian of Norwich - *Revelations of Divine Love*, [ed. Wolters], London: Penguin, 1966

Kempe, Margery - *The Book of Margery Kempe* [ed. Windeatt], London: Penguin Classics, 1985

Merton, Thomas - *The Seven Storey Mountain*, San Francisco: Harper & Row, 1984

Pseudo-Dionysius - *Pseudo-Dionysius: The Complete Works* [trans Luibheid], Classics of Western Spirituality, New York: Paulist Press, 1987

Rolle, Richard - *A Form of Living*, in *The English Writings* [ed. Allen], Classics of Western Spirituality, London: SPCK, 1989

Rolle, Richard - *The Fire of Love* [ed. C. Wolters], London: Penguin Classics, 1972

Teresa of Avila - *The Interior Castle*, Classics of Western Spirituality, London: SPCK, 1979

Underhill, E. - *Practical Mysticism: A Little Book for Normal People*, London: Dent, 1919

Secondary Sources

Burrows, R. - *Ascent to Love: The Spiritual Teaching of St John of the Cross*, London: DLT, 1987

Corduan, Winfried - *Mysticism: An Evangelical Option?* Grand Rapids: Zondervan, 1991

Cox, M. - *A Handbook of Christian Mysticism* Part 1, Crucible, 1986

Demarest, Bruce - *Satisfy your Soul: Restoring the Heart of Christian Spirituality*, Colorado Springs: NavPress, 1999

Ferguson, S. B. - *Christian Spirituality: Five Views of Sanctification*, Illinois: IVP, 1988

Foster, Richard *Celebration of Discipline: The Path to Spiritual Growth* revised edition; San Francisco: Harper & Row, 1988

Fowler, James - *Faithful Change* Nashville: Abingdon, 1996

Fry, Alison - *Learning from the English Mystics*, Cambridge: Grove Spirituality Series no.68, 1999

Harton, F. P. - *The Elements of the Spiritual Life* London: SPCK, 1932

Houston, James - *Gott Lieben und seine Gebote halten,* Basle: Brunner Verlag, 1991

James, W. - *The Varieties of Religious Experience,* Longmans, 1922

Leech, K. - *Soul Friend: A Study of Spirituality,* Sheldon Press, 1977

McGrath, Alister - *Christian Spirituality,* Oxford: Blackwell, 1999

Miles, M. R. - *The Image and Practice of Holiness,* London:SCM, 1988

Muto, S. A. - *John of the Cross for Today,* Indiana: Ave Maria Press

Nouwen, H. - *The Way of The Heart: Desert Spirituality and Contemporary Ministry* London: DLT, 1981

Nygren, A - *Eros and Agape,* [trans Watson] London, SPCK, 1953

Owen, John - *The Work of the Holy Spirit in Prayer,* orig. pubd. 1682; in *The Works of John Owen* [ed. Gould], vol 4, Edinburgh: Banner of Truth Trust, 1967

Pearce, J. F. D. - *A Critique of Spirituality,* Oxford: Latimer study no. 52

Rahner K. - *The Theological Investigations 3,* London: DLT, 1967

Raikes, Marian - *Presenting Everyone Mature,* [Orthos 21], Blackpool: Fellowship of Word and Spirit, 2004

Raiter, Mike - *Stirrings of the Soul,* London: Good Book Co, 2003

Runcorn, D. - *Space for God* London: Daybreak, 1990

Smith, M - *An Introduction to Mysticism,* London: Sheldon, 1977

Underhill, E. - *Mystics of the Church,* Cambridge: Clarke, 1925

Underhill, E. - *Mysticism,* London: Methuen, 1967

Wenham, G.J. *Word Biblical Commentary* on Genesis 16-50, Dallas: Word, 1994

Williams, Rowan *The Wound of Knowledge,* DLT, revised edition 1990

Catechism of the Catholic Church

The Essential Catholic Handbook, [ed. S. Finnegan] Canterbury Press, 1997

The New SCM Dictionary of Christian Spirituality, [ed. Sheldrake] London: SCM, 2005

B. Robertson, *What is a Christian mystic?* On the website www.christianmystics.com

www.pastornet.net.au/jmm/spir

www.jesuits.ca/spirituality/examen.htm

Latimer Studies